Extraordinary Chambers

David Wiener

A Samuel French Acting Edition

SAMUELFRENCH.COM
SAMUELFRENCH-LONDON.CO.UK

Copyright © 2015 by David Wiener
All Rights Reserved

EXTRAORDINARY CHAMBERS is fully protected under the copyright laws of the United States of America, the British Commonwealth, including Canada, and all other countries of the Copyright Union. All rights, including professional and amateur stage productions, recitation, lecturing, public reading, motion picture, radio broadcasting, television and the rights of translation into foreign languages are strictly reserved.

ISBN 978-0-573-70369-0

www.SamuelFrench.com
www.SamuelFrench-London.co.uk

For Production Enquiries

United States and Canada
Info@SamuelFrench.com
1-866-598-8449

United Kingdom and Europe
Plays@SamuelFrench-London.co.uk
020-7255-4302

Each title is subject to availability from Samuel French, depending upon country of performance. Please be aware that *EXTRAORDINARY CHAMBERS* may not be licensed by Samuel French in your territory. Professional and amateur producers should contact the nearest Samuel French office or licensing partner to verify availability.

CAUTION: Professional and amateur producers are hereby warned that *EXTRAORDINARY CHAMBERS* is subject to a licensing fee. Publication of this play(s) does not imply availability for performance. Both amateurs and professionals considering a production are strongly advised to apply to Samuel French before starting rehearsals, advertising, or booking a theatre. A licensing fee must be paid whether the title(s) is presented for charity or gain and whether or not admission is charged. Professional/Stock licensing fees are quoted upon application to Samuel French.

No one shall make any changes in this title(s) for the purpose of production. No part of this book may be reproduced, stored in a retrieval system, or transmitted in any form, by any means, now known or yet to be invented, including mechanical, electronic, photocopying, recording, videotaping, or otherwise, without the prior written permission of the publisher. No one shall upload this title(s), or part of this title(s), to any social media websites.

For all enquiries regarding motion picture, television, and other media rights, please contact Samuel French.

MUSIC USE NOTE

Licensees are solely responsible for obtaining formal written permission from copyright owners to use copyrighted music in the performance of this play and are strongly cautioned to do so. If no such permission is obtained by the licensee, then the licensee must use only original music that the licensee owns and controls. Licensees are solely responsible and liable for all music clearances and shall indemnify the copyright owners of the play(s) and their licensing agent, Samuel French, against any costs, expenses, losses and liabilities arising from the use of music by licensees. Please contact the appropriate music licensing authority in your territory for the rights to any incidental music.

IMPORTANT BILLING AND CREDIT REQUIREMENTS

If you have obtained performance rights to this title, please refer to your licensing agreement for important billing and credit requirements.

EXTRAORDINARY CHAMBERS was originally produced by
Geffen Playhouse,
Gilbert Cates, Producing Director; Randall Arney, Artistic Director;
Ken Novice, Managing Director

EXTRAORDINARY CHAMBERS was first produced by Geffen Playhouse (Gilbert Cates, Producing Director; Randall Arney, Artistic Director; Ken Novice, Managing Director) on May 24, 2011 in Los Angeles, CA. The performance was directed by Pam McKinnon, with sets by Myung Hi Cho, costumes by Alex Jaeger, lighting by Lap Chi Chu, and sound by Vincent Olivieri. The Production Stage Manager was Young Ji. The cast was as follows:

MARA	Marin Hinkle
CARTER	Mather Zickel
SOPOAN	Greg Watanabe
DR. HENG	Francois Chau
ROM CHANG	Kimiko Gelman

CHARACTERS

MARA – Female, American, Late 30s
CARTER – Male, American, Late 30s
SOPOAN – Male, Khmer, 40s
DR. HENG – Male, Khmer, 60s
ROM CHANG – Female, Khmer, 40s

AUTHOR'S NOTES

Lines spoken in Khmer or French are indicated in bold.* The English translation of these lines is indicated by the bold, italicized text in brackets following the spoken line.

    HENG. Chenh tou! *[Get out of my house!]*

---

* Lines in Khmer are spelled phonetically.

ACT I

(A hotel room in Phnom Penh, Cambodia. **CARTER** *switches on the light as he enters with* **MARA**. *She heads straight for the bathroom offstage. The sound of running water.)*

CARTER. It's nice.

(A toilet flushes. **CARTER** *inspects the room. He checks for a dial tone on the phone. He turns on the TV. We hear the laugh track and wacky sound effects of an Indonesian sitcom. He turns it off.)*

(To **MARA** *offstage:)*

This is nice, don't you think?

(No response. He goes to the bathroom door.)

How's the bathroom?
(Beat.) Sweetie? You all right? Mara?

*(***MARA** *emerges from the bathroom.)*

How is it?

MARA. How is what?

CARTER. The bathroom.

(She begins sorting through her purse.)

Mara?

MARA. It's amazing Carter. It's beyond words –

CARTER. Okay –

MARA. You see they've constructed this magnificent porcelain dais –

CARTER. All right –

MARA. Near to which, is positioned a roll of papery material which must have been used in the ancient Cambodian practice of mummification.

CARTER. I get it. You're tired. Excuse me.

(CARTER heads for the bathroom.)

MARA. It's an archeologist's dream in there baby.

(She begins to undress. The sound of running water. Carter comes out of the bathroom. A beat.)

CARTER. It's nice.

MARA. Can we please just go to sleep?

CARTER. It's the middle of the afternoon.

MARA. It's the middle of the night.

CARTER. I think if we just push through –

MARA. No.

CARTER. We'll be on their time.

MARA. I don't want to be on their time. My back is killing me. I'm exhausted.

CARTER. You didn't sleep on the plane?

MARA. No.

CARTER. I did.

MARA. I know.

CARTER. Took one of those pills.

MARA. I know.

CARTER. You didn't take a pill?

MARA. No.

CARTER. Why not?

MARA. Carter.

CARTER. All right, but Sopoan's coming with the bags.

MARA. Who?

CARTER. Our guide, sweetie. Sopoan.

MARA. Tell him to bring them in the morning.

CARTER. But I told him to bring them now.

(A beat. MARA goes into the bathroom again. CARTER opens the French doors that lead to the modest balcony. He surveys the view. Something outside catches his

attention. **CARTER** *retrieves his camera from his bag. He begins taking pictures.* **MARA** *re-enters in a robe.)*

CARTER. Look at this. Sweetie. Look.

MARA. I'll look tomorrow.

CARTER. You have to look now.

MARA. Why?

CARTER. Just look.

(MARA crosses to the French doors.)

MARA. What am I looking at?

CARTER. The old guy, right there. Do you see? Look at this old guy.

MARA. Where?

CARTER. *(Taking photos:)* Right there. Edge of the canal there. Behind the house. What is he doing? Do you see?

MARA. Oh. Yes.

CARTER. What is he doing? Is he praying?

MARA. No.

CARTER. But he's like… What is he… Oh.

(He lowers his camera.)

MARA. Save that one for me.

CARTER. I guess they don't have plumbing there.

MARA. I'll use it for the Christmas card.

CARTER. Why don't you get some sleep sweetie.

MARA. Thank you.

(MARA drops her robe and gets into bed. She rolls over. Short pause.)

(CARTER sits on the bed beside her and strokes her arm. Pause.)

CARTER. Mara?

(Beat.) Baby…

MARA. Mhhmm?

CARTER. I'm glad you came.

MARA. I smell smoke.

CARTER. I think it's harvest time.

MARA. No, I smell smoke, like cigarette smoke.

(Suddenly wracked with pain:) OW – OW! OW!

CARTER. Spasm?

MARA. OW! Son of a – Fuck!

CARTER. Rub?

(He does.)

MARA. OW!

CARTER. No?

MARA. OW!

CARTER. Yes? Rub? No rub?

MARA. Ow…

CARTER. Okay, you're okay, breathe.

MARA. Owww –

(There's a knock at the door.)

CARTER. Okay. I'm here. You're –

(More knocking.)

Shit. Breathe. I got it. Just – you're okay.

MARA. *(The pain subsiding:)* Jesus…

(CARTER exits.)

Tell him to leave them in the hall. Carter.

(SOPOAN, a Khmer man in his 40s, enters with two suitcases. He's followed by CARTER.)

SOPOAN. *(Entering:)* Where would you like suitcase Mr. Carter?

CARTER. That's perfect, right there. **Aw kun** Sopoan.

SOPOAN. Unjuhn Mr. Carter.

(Noticing MARA, a whisper:)

Oh. Is Miss Mara sleeping?

CARTER. Not really.

SOPOAN. Are you sleeping Miss Mara?

MARA. No.

SOPOAN. Okay. I will get the other.

CARTER. Aw kun Sopoan.

SOPOAN. Unjuhn Mr. Carter.

   (**SOPOAN** *exits.*)

CARTER. He's sweet, isn't he?

MARA. Just tell him to leave them in the hall.

CARTER. What do you want me to do?

MARA. I want you to tell him to leave them in the –

   (**SOPOAN** *enters with more bags.*)

SOPOAN. So sorry. Excuse me.

CARTER. Aw kun Sopoan.

SOPOAN. Unjuhn Mr. Carter.

   (*To* **MARA***:*) He speak very good Khmer.

MARA. Yes.

SOPOAN. Are you comfortable in the bed now Miss Mara?

MARA. Yes. Thank you, Sopon.

CARTER. Sopoan.

MARA. Sopon.

SOPOAN. Sopoan.

MARA. Sopon.

SOPOAN. Sopoan.

MARA. Uh huh. What did I say?

CARTER. You said *So-pon* Sweetie, but it's *So-pwan*. *Sopwan*.

MARA. Great. Okay.

SOPOAN. Tomorrow I will pick you up. We leave 900 hours, okay?

CARTER. That's perfect.

SOPOAN. You are comfortable in the bed?

MARA. Yes. Yes, I am comfortable in the bed.

CARTER. The bed is perfect. The bed is great.

   (*Beat.*)

MARA. So I guess that's it then.

SOPOAN. Okay. I see you in the morning.

CARTER. Thank you Sopoan. And thank you for sharing your beautiful country with us.

SOPOAN. Thank you for coming to Cambodia Mr. Carter.

CARTER. You are very welcome.

SOPOAN. Aw kun.

CARTER. Unjuhn.

SOPOAN. Ret'rei sues'day *[Good night]* Mr. Carter, Miss Mara.

CARTER. Ret'rei sues'day Sopoan.

(SOPOAN exits.)

I love that guy. Don't you love that guy?

MARA. Please shut up.

CARTER. What is with you?

MARA. I haven't slept in thirty eight hours. My shoulder is –

CARTER. Okay. Fine.

(Retrieving his book:) Maybe I'll go down to the pool.

MARA. Fine.

CARTER. You'll be all right here?

(No response.)

Good. You just sleep. We'll get up in the morning. We'll go for a walk maybe. It really is very beautiful here. It's very…green. Mara?

(No response.) I'm glad you came… It's going to be good for us. I think getting away is good. It's very green here.

(She rolls over. **CARTER** *watches her for a moment, then turns to go.)*

MARA. Do you have to be so God damned obsequious?

CARTER. What?

MARA. Obsequious.

CARTER. You're tired. You don't know what you mean.

MARA. I mean the fawning ridiculous things you say.

CARTER. I say ridiculous things?

MARA. Yes.

CARTER. Well thank you sweetie.

MARA. Don't do that.

CARTER. What? If trying to connect with you is –

MARA. Oh, this is like a romantic getaway now?

CARTER. Are you feeling neglected?

MARA. I'm feeling embarrassed.

CARTER. You have nothing to be embarrassed about.

MARA. I'm feeling embarrassed for you Carter. By you.

CARTER. Me?

MARA. Forget it. Read your book.

CARTER. I think I will.

(He opens his book. A beat. He closes it.)

Do you mean how I am with the locals? Is that what you mean?

MARA. Good night.

CARTER. No. No. Do you mean, showing some interest in another culture? You mean trying to learn their history? You mean speaking their language –

MARA. You don't speak their language.

CARTER. I speak some.

MARA. You can say like three things.

CARTER. I can say more than three.

MARA. Well I know you can say, "thank you." I know you can say that because you said it like sixty fucking times on the way from the airport.

CARTER. So I am polite. So I express some gratitude and respect and, and –

MARA. Aw kun for opening the door Sopon. **Aw kun** for speaking English Sopon –

CARTER. Sopoan.

MARA. I don't care.

CARTER. See that's your problem.

MARA. Aw kun for driving so carefully Sopon.

CARTER. I didn't say that.

MARA. Yes you did.

CARTER. Well those roads are – I mean, I couldn't drive here, could you? Could you drive here?

MARA. Did it occur to you that they may not like it?

CARTER. Like what?

MARA. You know, your whole, Ambassador of America routine.

CARTER. You mean my courtesy?

MARA. Whatever you call it. Maybe your little buddy doesn't like being treated like a child.

CARTER. I don't treat him like a child. I am polite. And I am considerate. And perhaps I'm a little too considerate in an effort to compensate for my wife who behaves like the queen of the fucking plantation –

MARA. I do not.

CARTER. Like everybody's working for her.

MARA. He does work for me.

CARTER. No. No Mara, he works for Doctor Heng. And for the next six days, he works for me. And I appreciate it. My God, what is with you?

MARA. I just... I would like it...if we could keep things professional.

(Short pause.)

CARTER. Do you have any idea what these people have been through?

MARA. I have an idea.

CARTER. They spent twenty-five years murdering twenty-five percent of their population. Can you imagine? And somehow, everywhere I look, these people are smiling. Have you noticed that? They know so much death, and they're just...

(Short pause.)

MARA. It's unsettling...

CARTER. I'm going down to the pool.

MARA. I don't like it here.

CARTER. Yes you do –

MARA. I –

CARTER. Yes you do. You like it here Mara. You wanted to come and you like it here.

MARA. Carter –

CARTER. And I like it here. And it is beautiful. And I like it. And you will not shit all over this. Because it is important. This is important to me. And you like it.

(Beat. He breathes.)

And I am going down to the pool.

MARA. Don't… Carter.

(He exits.)

Carter…

(Blackout.)

(Contained light up on **SOPOAN**. *He sits in a wooden chair.)*

SOPOAN. The termites built their nest on the roots of the tree outside our house. This was bad for the tree. But this was good for us. Because the termite pile many kilogram of mud to make their home. Beneath the nest is safe. Beneath the nest no shrapnel will penetrate and no one will come looking for you. This is where we dug.

(Beat.)

We met in École Miche. I receive always low marks in French speaking. This was bad for me as a student. But this was good for me because boys sometime need believable reason for talking to girls. And she was very excellent in speaking like the French. And she was beautiful. And I loved her very much. I do not maybe know how to say in English but, **Khnium pibak chet dol haeui**. She made sickness in my heart.

(Beat.)

On the first day of our marriage, my wife make offerings to our ancestor. On the second day, my wife decide the names for our children. On the third day of our marriage, she help me to dig the hole.

(Short pause. He composes himself.)

You are making record of this?

(Beat.)

The men come in the morning time. My wife take my spectacles from my face and throws them over the tin roof. This was bad for me because I could not see. This was good for me because CPK always execute anyone who wears glasses. Because glasses are for reading. Do you understand? The men come. My wife take my hand. She lead me down in the hole.

(Beat.)

For a very long time. I hear sounds. In the dark. I hear the termite in the mud above my head. All of them. A great blind nation. With one voice, asking to me, where is your shirt? And I didn't know. And the termite ask, where is your shoes? And I didn't know. And the termite ask, what is that sound? And I didn't know. And the termite ask, where is your wife? And I said, I think she went to find my glasses.

(Short pause.)

The termite tell me not to have sadness. You are not alone they say. You live in the earth and cannot see. You are one of us. Forget yourself Sopoan. Join us. Stay…

(Blackout.)

(A radio plays 1940s French be-bop. Lights up on the main room of a villa in Phnom Penh. Two shuttered French doors dominate the upstage wall. The plaster is peeling in places but the room is finely furnished. The desk, table, chairs, etc. are all nineteenth century and French. The table is cluttered with the remnants of a party: cigarette butts, dirty glasses and several empty bottles of Bordeaux. **SOPOAN** *stands near the entrance. He studies the scene. A beat.)*

SOPOAN. **Tium reap suor?** *[Hello?]*

(He crosses to the radio and turns it off. A beat.)

Mean neak na nau te? *[Hello? Is anyone here?]*

*(***SOPOAN*** goes to the upstage doors and opens them, revealing the balcony that overlooks the street. Bougainvillea spills over its iron rails.* **SOPOAN** *is airing out the room when* **CARTER** *enters, followed by* **MARA.***)*

CARTER. Looks like someone had a party.

SOPOAN. Oh, Mr. Carter. You should please wait in the van.

CARTER. We were actually a bit uncomfortable in the van.

SOPOAN. Driver will turn on air con for you.

CARTER. Yes, It's just that I think we prefer to be out of the van.

MARA. What Carter means is that it wasn't so much the heat in the van, as it was the men with the guns outside of the van that made us uncomfortable.

CARTER. I didn't say that.

(To **SOPOAN***:)*

That's not what I said.

MARA. I didn't say you said it Carter. I'm saying it. Me.

CARTER. Yes sweetie. But I don't think it's fair to give the impression that I was necessarily uncomfortable for the same reason you were uncomfortable.

SOPOAN. Everyone is very safe here.

CARTER. Yes. We know that Sopoan.

MARA. We do?

CARTER. I didn't notice the guns.

MARA. Oh really?

SOPOAN. You please wait in the van Mr. Carter.

CARTER. I'm sure you'll grant me Mara that it's possible for two people to be uncomfortable for different reasons in the same van.

MARA. I do grant you that. My reason is the guns.

CARTER. Mara.

MARA. Carter.

CARTER. You're offending our host.

MARA. You mean him?

   (*To* **SOPOAN***:*)

   Are you offended? Am I offending you?

SOPOAN. No Miss Mara.

MARA. He's not offended.

SOPOAN. It is important you please wait in the van please.

CARTER. He's being nice. His sense of propriety won't allow him to embarrass you.

SOPOAN. Mr. Carter please.

MARA. His what?

CARTER. Propriety. His sense of what is proper. That's what this is. Though I shouldn't expect you to –

   (**HENG**, *a Khmer man in his 60s, enters with a revolver.*)

HENG. Chenh tou! *[Get out of my house!]*

CARTER. Holy shit!

HENG. Chenh tou!

   (**CARTER** *freezes.*)

SOPOAN. (*To* **HENG***:*) **Kom tveu onh cheung!** *[No, no don't shoot!]*

HENG. Khnium min chlaeui te, sdap ban te? *[I won't answer any questions! Do you hear me?]*

CARTER. (*Overlapping:*) Holy shit! Holy shit!

SOPOAN. **Dak choh dak choh lauk.** *[Put it down sir.]*

HENG. *(To* **SOPOAN***:)* **Ech eng noam ke mok phteah anh?** *[You bring them to my house?]*

MARA. *(Overlapping:)* Don't shoot!

SOPOAN. **Lauk yul chhro lom haeui.** *[You have the wrong idea.]*

CARTER. Holy shit!

HENG. *(To* **CARTER***:)* **Khnium min men chia ao kret chun te. Auk khmean sit mok ti ni te!** *[I'm not the criminal! You are the criminal! You have no authority here!]*

MARA. Oh my god. Say something!

CARTER. *(Searching for the words:)* Uhhh, uhhh, uhhhh, uhhh –

HENG. **Chhab niyeai phleam!** *[Speak lackey dog!]*

MARA. For Christ sake Carter!

CARTER. Uhh – **Som kom hel pek.**

(A beat. **HENG** *lowers the gun.)*

HENG. **Tha mech?** *[What?]*

CARTER. I don't really, uh – **Pon – Pon neung hel?**

HENG. Not…so spicy?

(To **SOPOAN***:)* **Ke lop te deng?** *[Is he an idiot?]*

SOPOAN. **Koat chun cheat a me ri cang.** *[He's American.]*

HENG. Oh.

SOPOAN. **Koat chia chiang turasap.** *[From the phone company.]*

*(***HENG** *processes this information. Short pause.)*

HENG. Hello… Hello.

CARTER. Hi.

HENG. I am very sorry. I thought you were someone else.

CARTER. No.

HENG. You are from the phone company?

CARTER. Yes.

(Beat.)

Yes. I'm Carter Dean. From PanaTel.

HENG. Of course. I am very good friends with your predecessor, Mr. Lawrence. How is Brian?

CARTER. Oh, uh, Good. I think he's –

HENG. Stephanie and the children are well?

CARTER. I think so.

HENG. *(Seeing* **MARA***:)* Tell me, who is your lovely colleague?

CARTER. Oh, no, this is –

MARA. I'm Mara.

(**HENG** *takes her hand.*)

HENG. I am honored to meet you. I am Doctor Heng.

MARA. Nice to meet you.

CARTER. Mara is my wife.

HENG. Oh?

(To **SOPOAN***:)*

Pit te? [Is this true?]

SOPOAN. Bat tean. *[Yes.]*

HENG. *(To* **CARTER***:)* I see why you are married to your work.

CARTER. Oh. No, Mara doesn't work for the company. She just came along.

HENG. I see.

CARTER. We thought it would be kind of a working vacation. It seemed like a good chance to get away.

(A beat. **HENG** *laughs.* **CARTER** *manages to laugh along.)*

HENG. *(Beat.)* Well. Welcome to Cambodia. Please excuse the mess.

(**SOPOAN** *begins tidying the room.*)

(Calling offstage:) **Ca vas. Tu peux sortire. C'est seulement des Americains. Ils sont inoffensifs.** *[It's all right. You can come out. It's only Americans.]*

(To **MARA***:)*

Had I known you were coming I would have arranged properly. Sopoan has done us all a terrible disservice by failing to remind me of your visit.

SOPOAN. I am very sorry Mr. Carter. I am very sorry Miss Mara.

HENG. He is very sorry. Sopoan is kind but incompetent.

(To **MARA***:)*

Please, sit down and allow us to serve you.

CARTER. I'm afraid Mara can't stay.

HENG. Of course she can.

MARA. Actually, Sopoan was going to take me to see Angkor Wat.

HENG. Angkor is many miles away.

MARA. I was told we could be there this afternoon.

HENG. Oh yes, you can be there this afternoon. And you can spend a few hours among the tourists. The Germans. The Dutch. You can take your pictures to show your friends. "Look, that is me, and in the background there is the greatest artistic achievement in the history of mankind." But I look at you Mara and I think that you are a person who lives deeply in things. I want to believe that you would rather go at dawn – that you would rather go alone to watch the sun rise on Suryavaram's city without a soul in sight. With only the silence of the stone.

And no person or thing to convince you that you are not there, then, when this was still Vishnu's world. I want to believe that you would like that.

MARA. I believe I would.

HENG. Then it shall be.

(To **SOPOAN***:)*

Na eng sdap ban te? *[Did you get that?]*

SOPOAN. Bat tean. *[Yes.]*

MARA. I'm sorry, you can do that?

HENG. I can do anything.

CARTER. That is very generous sir. But it's really not necessary.

HENG. Perhaps not necessary for a man who brings his wife to Phnom Penh when she obviously belongs in Paris.

(Beat.)

After all, there's no use in being a man in my position if I cannot do a favor for my friends.

(To MARA:)

So, you will go to Angkor Mara. But not today.

CARTER. Thank you Doctor Heng.

HENG. It is I that am grateful. It has been too long since we have had the right sort of guests. You will sit please.

(HENG pulls out a chair for MARA who sits. CARTER takes a seat and opens his briefcase. ROM CHANG, a Khmer woman, 40, enters.)

Ah te voila. Bonjour ma petite fleur. *[Ah, here you are. Good morning my flower.]*

ROM CHANG. C'est l'apres midi. *[It's afternoon.]*

HENG. Tu peux nous apporter du vin pour nos invites si vous plait? *[Would you bring our guests some wine?]*

ROM CHANG. Les Americains ne boivent pas durant la journee. *[Americans don't drink in the daytime.]*

HENG. Meme pas un excellent Bordeaux? *[Not even an exceptional Bordeaux?]*

ROM CHANG. Ils sont sensibles aux apparences. Je pense que tu devrais faire meme. *[They worry about appearances. Maybe you should too.]*

HENG. Tu sais je suis trop vieux pour avoir peur du ridicule. *[You know I'm too old to worry about appearing ridiculous.]*

(To MARA and CARTER:)

May we offer you a drink?

CARTER. I'd love a water.

ROM CHANG. Tu vois? *[See?]*

MARA. J'aimerais bien gouter ce Bordeaux. *[I'd love to try that Bordeaux.]*

(Beat.)

HENG. **Vous parlez Francais?** *[You speak French?]*

MARA. **Qu'elles que mots.** *[A few words.]*

HENG. How did I know?

CARTER. I'm sorry, what? He knew what?

HENG. *(Still to* **MARA***:)* **Je croix que c'est plus que "qu'elles que mot". Vous avez passe' du temps en france?** *[I think it's more than a few words. Have you spent time in France?]*

MARA. **J'avais un appartement dans le Quartier Saint-Germain-des-Prés.** *[I had a flat in Saint-Germain-des-Prés.]*

HENG. **Vraiment?** *[Is that so?]*

CARTER. Mara speaks excellent French.

MARA. **J'ai etudie a L'École des Beaux-Arts pour un an.** *[I studied at École des Beaux-Arts for a year.]*

HENG. **Biensur, j'aurais du savoir. Mois j'etes etudiand as Paris aussi. Quel est ta medium?** *[Of course, I should have known. I was a student in Paris as well. What's your medium?]*

MARA. **Sculture.** *[Sculpture.]*

(**ROM CHANG** *enters with the wine. She places four glasses on the table.*)

HENG. **Magnifique!** *[Magnificent!]*

(To **ROM CHANG***:)*

Tu entends ca? *[Are you hearing this?]*

ROM CHANG. **Oui.** *[Yes.]*

MARA. **Mais je suis pas vraiment une artiste. Je pensais que j'en etais un … Mais ca a dure seulement un an.** *[But I'm not really an artist. I thought I was but… It was only for a year.]*

CARTER. I actually don't speak any French.

HENG. My apologies Carter. We are being rude.

CARTER. No. It's fine. It's great. Mara's my ambassador, you know. We go to a restaurant, I just hand her the menu.

HENG. I see.

CARTER. She went to art school there. In Paris.

HENG. So she tells me. Sculpture.

CARTER. Right. But, anyway, lucky for me, she came back.

HENG. Very lucky I would say. A woman goes to Paris, she so often disappears.

CARTER. Disappears?

HENG. I don't mean that she vanishes from existence of course. I only mean that to be young – to be young and alive in the true center of the world, drowning in ideas – to be intoxicated by art, by that passion. A young woman is naturally changed by this. She experiences an opening of herself that makes her entirely… unrecognizable.

(*To* **MARA***:*)

T'es d'accord? *[Don't you agree?]*

MARA. Oui.

(**ROM CHANG** *pours* **CARTER** *a glass of water.*)

HENG. But fortunately for you Carter, she returned.

CARTER. Yes well, that was before we met. Mara went through her artsy phase in college.

MARA. My what?

HENG. Oh I see.

CARTER. Yes. So um…

(*To* **ROM CHANG***:*)

Sorry. Do you have bottled water?

(**ROM CHANG** *looks to* **HENG**. *He nods. She exits again.* **HENG** *goes to get the wine from the table. Short pause.*)

HENG. You know, you should not listen to me. I get nostalgic when the light is like this. I am certain I exaggerate the glory of my student days.

MARA. What did you study?

HENG. I would not bore you with the details of my doctoral thesis. The academic facets of an education are secondary, don't you think? Just the ideas of dead men repeated by old men.

(**HENG** *pops the cork on the Bordeaux.*)

But I was a young man in Paris. We were all young men. We grew our own ideas.

(**HENG** *pours the wine.*)

MARA. This smells delicious.

HENG. You must give it some time. It is very very shy.

(*Inhaling:*)

Leather and iron give way to…grass…a faint organic hint of soil…copper…perhaps even blood. When you taste it, you will understand why Hitler diverted his most elite commandos from the invasion of Paris and sent them directly to Bordeaux.

CARTER. He did?

HENG. Yes.

CARTER. For this?

HENG. Well I don't think anyone can really say Carter. But we know the French gave up their Gypsies and their Jews. They hid the wine.

(**CARTER** *looks at his wine.*)

Please. Drink.

(**CARTER** *and* **MARA** *drink.*)

CARTER. (*Uncertain:*) Mmmm…

MARA. Oh wow. That is fabulous.

CARTER. Mara's half Jewish.

HENG. Oh?

MARA. What does that have to do with anything?

CARTER. Well – I was just – forget it. Look, Doctor Heng, it is really just lovely for you to entertain us here like this.

HENG. It is my honor.

CARTER. You've been very generous and I really hate to mix business with pleasure –

HENG. So do I.

CARTER. Right. But you see I'm going to have get on a call tonight with Brian and some of the folks in New York –

HENG. They will want to know if I am amenable.

CARTER. Well, if I had something to tell them, it would be really great.

HENG. Tell them I look forward to improving the lives of all Cambodians through the magic of American commerce.

CARTER. *(Producing some papers:)* That's great. I put together a little presentation actually. Very exciting, I think. If we could get something in writing…it would be would be very –

HENG. *(To* **MARA***:)* There are no Nazis here today.

MARA. Pardon?

HENG. *(Re:* **MARA***'s empty glass:)* You drink as if you believe they are coming to steal your wine.

MARA. Oh I… Oh gosh – I didn't realize I… Sorry.

HENG. Nonsense. There is nothing to forgive.

(To **CARTER***:)*

Your wife is wise to take fully from the cup. It is as in life I think. Those that sip cautiously risk leaving Bordeaux in the glass. Don't you agree?

CARTER. Well sure. Carpe diem and all that.

*(***HENG** *gives little toast to* **CARTER** *and drinks his own glass dry.)*

HENG. *(To* **MARA***:)* More?

MARA. Thank you.

*(***HENG** *pours. He sits back in his chair.* **ROM CHANG** *enters and gives* **CARTER** *his water.)*

CARTER. Oh thanks. **Aw Kun** uh… I'm sorry I didn't get –

(To **HENG***:)*

What is your maid's name?

HENG. Her name is Rom Chang.

CARTER. **Aw kun** Rom Chang.

HENG. And she is my wife.

CARTER. Is she? Ah, well... – I'm very uh –

(*To* **MARA**:)

Uh, how do you say –

MARA. Desolé. You say **desolé**.

CARTER. (*To* **ROM CHANG**:) **Desolé**. I am sorry. I –

ROM CHANG. It's okay.

CARTER. And you speak English.

ROM CHANG. So do you.

CARTER. You know I was confused there because –

MARA. Carter was confused.

HENG. My wife is young, yes?

CARTER. No. I mean, yes, she's young – but she's not – I mean she's younger – but not –

MARA. It's very nice to meet you Rom Chang. I'm Mara.

ROM CHANG. The Parisian sculptor, I heard.

(*Short pause.*)

MARA. You have a lovely home.

ROM CHANG. Except for the men with the guns, of course.

MARA. You know, I'm sure it's entirely necessary for a man in your husband's position.

ROM CHANG. What is your husband's position?

MARA. Sorry?

ROM CHANG. Do you know?

(*Re:* **CARTER**:) What does he do?

HENG. My dear, please.

MARA. He works for a phone company.

CARTER. I work for PanaTel.

(*Off* **ROM CHANG**'s *look:*)

You know, PanaTel. "We put your world within reach."

ROM CHANG. What does that mean?

CARTER. Mean?

ROM CHANG. Yes.

CARTER. Oh. Well, what it means is that in this increasingly fragmented and fast-paced world, what we risk losing are the most basic, most human aspects of our communication. So when we say, "we put your world within reach", what we are really saying is, we're going to provide you with the tools, and the network, and the solutions necessary for you to, to…to just uh…to…

MARA. To reach out and touch someone.

ROM CHANG. Touch someone?

CARTER. Yes, right. But, you know, with your voice.

ROM CHANG. *(To* **HENG***:)* **Eng lu te? Koat min men chiang "phone company". Ta-e koat mok tveu ey?** *[Did you hear that? He doesn't work for any "phone company". Why have they come?]*

HENG. Pon neung ban heui. Eng thveu ke teuh toal heuy. *[Stop it. You're going to make them uncomfortable.]*

ROM CHANG. Khnium te thel dial tueh toal. Neh kueh tai. *[I'm the one that's uncomfortable. You should be.]*

MARA. I'm sorry, is something wrong?

ROM CHANG. We already have phones. We have Chinese phones. We have Russian phones. Vietnamese phones. We had French phones but they all are buried now.

HENG. You must pardon my wife, she is conditioned to be suspicious.

ROM CHANG. Of suspicious people.

HENG. Pon neung ban heui. *[Stop it.]*

(To **MARA***:)*

What she means to say is that sometimes, in our country, it is hard to know whom to trust.

CARTER. I really do work at PanaTel. Here uh… I have a card.

(He slides his business card to **ROM CHANG** *who doesn't look at it.)*

ROM CHANG. They dropped two million tons of bombs here. In secret. Do you think the CIA could manage to make a business card?

MARA. CIA?

CARTER. I'm not in the CIA.

MARA. *(Laughing:)* The CIA? Carter? You must be – No. No. I assure you, Carter is not in the CIA.

(To **CARTER***:)*

You're not in the CIA.

CARTER. No.

MARA. He's just a business man.

HENG. Forgive us. These are strange times.

MARA. Of course.

ROM CHANG. It has always been strange times here.

MARA. I understand.

ROM CHANG. You do not, understand.

(Short pause.)

MARA. No. You're right. I…

(Short pause.)

I just mean that you can trust me. Us.

CARTER. I work for a phone company.

ROM CHANG. *(To* **MARA***:)* Give me your hand.

MARA. Sorry?

ROM CHANG. Give me your hand.

HENG. *(To* **ROM CHANG.***:)* **Kom tveu onh cheung rom chang. [*Don't Rom Chang.*]**

(Short pause.)

ROM CHANG. Your hand.

(A pause. **MARA** *tentatively extends her hand across the table.* **ROM CHANG** *encloses it with both of hers. She looks into* **MARA**. *A long pause.)*

ROM CHANG. You have pain.

MARA. Pain? No.
ROM CHANG. I help you.
MARA. Oh. No. That's okay I...
ROM CHANG. Deep breath.

> (**MARA**, *self-conscious, looks to* **CARTER**.)

Do you trust me? Deep Breath.

> (*A beat.* **MARA** *inhales.*)

MARA. I don't know what you – oh my...

> (**ROM CHANG** *presses her fingers into the flesh of* **MARA**'s *arm.*)

ROM CHANG. Better.
MARA. Oh...

> (**MARA** *inhales.*)

ROM CHANG. And here.

> (**ROM CHANG** *moves her hand up* **MARA**'s *arm.*)

And here, yes?

MARA. Yes.
ROM CHANG. Deep breath.

> (**MARA** *inhales.*)

ROM CHANG. And here.
MARA. Oh my God.
ROM CHANG. Deep breath.
CARTER. *(To* **HENG**.:*)* What is she doing?
MARA. Oh my God... What is that?

> (*She trembles.*)

> (*Lights shift – WE HEAR CHURNING SURF, VOICES, A FLUTTERING OF WINGS.*)

What is that?

> (*Beginning to weep:*)

What are you doing to me?

ROM CHANG. Where is the child?
CARTER. What?
MARA. Please…oh…oh my God Carter… I can smell his hair.
ROM CHANG. Deep breath.
   (Blackout.)

(The Hotel Room. **MARA** *stands in the center of the room, facing the bathroom door.* **MARA***'s clothes are sweat-stained from her trip to the jungle.)*

MARA. It was astonishing. So beautiful. You wouldn't have believed it… We should go. I mean, you should go. I'll go with you. I don't mind going again. I'd like to. Before we leave. It's really something you have to see. Carter?

(The toilet flushes. A beat. **MARA** *crosses to her pack, unzips it, and produces a stack of Polaroids.)*

Carter?

CARTER. *(Offstage:)* Just give me a sec.

(The sound of running water. **MARA** *takes the Polaroids and places them on the night stand.)*

MARA. It's another world. Ancient and – They had 250,000 artisans working for…a really long time. There's bas-relief for miles. Buddhas and…

(She picks up the Polaroids and positions them, more prominently, on the desk.)

…Golden Buddhas. I must have shot a hundred pictures. And Sopoan. He took the camera and… The man has a gift. Really captured it all. Knew the history… Maybe we could take a few days. You know, after you're done with your deal or… Carter?

*(***MARA*** picks up the photos again and quickly, but thoughtfully, shuffles their order.* **CARTER** *comes out of the bathroom. He's shirtless, drying his face with a towel.)*

CARTER. It was nice, huh?

MARA. Amazing.

*(***MARA*** watches as* **CARTER** *combs his hair in the mirror.)*

I tried to call you.

CARTER. Had my phone off. Didn't want any interruptions, you know?

MARA. Right.

(In the mirror, his eyes go to hers. A beat.)

CARTER. You look good.

MARA. No. I'm a mess.

CARTER. I mean, you look good. You know, like, happy.

MARA. Oh.

CARTER. I'm glad you had a good day. You deserve a good day.

(He crosses to her and takes her in his arms.)

MARA. I'm all sweaty.

CARTER. Don't really care.

(He kisses her face, then her neck.)

MARA. Carter.

CARTER. You didn't ask how my day was.

MARA. How was your day?

(He kisses her again, dipping her like a leading man.)

MARA. Wow. So. Good?

CARTER. I'm not going to lie to you. Was I nervous? Yes. Did I feel my career and possibly my future at this company hanging in the balance of a single presentation? Yes I did.

MARA. You did?

CARTER. I did. It's been a long time since I've – I maybe did wonder if I still had it, you know. Because, it's different now. That's what Brian will tell you. He'll give you the Powerpoint bullshit. He does it from a script.

MARA. Oh.

CARTER. I know, right? And there I am. I'm flipping these slides. I'm following the stupid script and I can plainly see I'm losing them.

MARA. Oh.

CARTER. The guy from the ministry is there, with his guys. And Heng's wife, who I am completely convinced hates my guts, is talking in Cambodian – It was very stressful. I'm sweating through my shirt and...and then I realize...where I am.

MARA. Where?

CARTER. I am in the jungle. I am standing in the undiscovered world. I am communing with people who still believe in magic. And Heng, he's like this – It's hard to describe. Some sort of poet, statesman, shaman. Would you get me a drink?

(MARA goes to the mini-bar and pours a drink.)

And I think he may be a great man. And I think I may be a great man, because I turn off the projector. And I look in their eyes and we just begin to talk. I tell them that this isn't about call-centers or regional revenue halos or even money.

(MARA brings CARTER the drink.)

Thank you. I tell them that this is about the last, most powerful kind of sorcery. I tell the Minister that I can help him change lives, save lives. Like what gods do. And I... I believe every single word I say Mara. Like I used to.

MARA. Oh.

CARTER. And it's coming out of my mouth like a poem and... God, I wish I could remember what I fucking said.

(CARTER laughs a little to himself and drinks.)

MARA. And?

(A beat.)

CARTER. And. It's a done deal.

(She embraces him.)

MARA. I'm very proud of you.

CARTER. You are?

MARA. Yes. I am very proud.

(She kisses him. Their kiss becomes deeper. It's tentative in the way of first times and long absences. MARA's hand

slides beneath his shirt. He pulls her hips closer. Then he pulls away.)

CARTER. I remember. I said, there can be no evil where there is prosperity.

MARA. That's nice.

CARTER. And I look over. And I swear to God, that little witch has tears in her eyes. I have to call Brian.

MARA. Carter.

CARTER. I'm sorry sweetie. I just... He left me this urgent message.

(**CARTER** *dials his cell.*)

MARA. I tried to call you –

CARTER. I know and I want to hear all about your trip but I have to catch Brian before –

(Into phone:)

Hey Jenny... Who do you think this is?

(Laughs:)

That's because I'm in Cambodia. No – Hey Jenny, is he in?

(Short pause.)

Of course he is... Well I think you better go get him... Yup.
Oh, I'm pretty sure he won't mind...

(To **MARA***:)*

In a meeting, my ass.

(A pause. **CARTER** *notices* **MARA***'s Polaroids.)*

CARTER. These from today?

MARA. Yes.

(**CARTER** *picks up the pictures and begins flipping through them.*)

CARTER. I don't know why you use this old thing. We have the digital.

MARA. Sopoan insisted.

CARTER. Insisted on Polaroid? That's odd.

MARA. He said he likes having something to hold.

CARTER. He took these?

MARA. Most.

CARTER. They stopped making the film, you know. That should tell you something.

MARA. What should that tell me?

CARTER. I don't know. It's the end of the analog world or – Wow. That is some temple.

MARA. It's really more like a city.

CARTER. So I see. Wow.

(*He looks through a few more.*)

CARTER. Sopoan?

MARA. Yes.

CARTER. Love that guy.

MARA. He's an artist.

CARTER. Is he?

MARA. Yes.

CARTER. Like you.

MARA. No, not like me.

CARTER. No?

MARA. I mean with the camera. He's very talented.

CARTER. Hm. I think I see what you mean.

MARA. He's had some training.

CARTER. Is that so.

MARA. That's what he says.

CARTER. Wow. That's –

(*Into phone:*)

Yeah. Yup. Still holding Jenny. In Cambodia. Waiting for – yup.

(**CARTER** *flips through a few more pictures. Short pause.*)

You should start sculpting again.

MARA. I don't think so.

CARTER. You used to like it. Remember? I'd come in. You'd be covered in plaster. I'd wash your hair. Do you remember? Mara?

(**MARA** *heads into the bathroom.*)

I'm serious. We could rent you a little studio. Somewhere over the river. We can afford it now. Especially now, you know. Perhaps I didn't communicate what this could mean for us. Mara? This means a lot. Whatever you want. I'm not talking South Hampton. But Catskills definitely. It means a lot.

(*Flipping through more pictures:*) Mara?

(*Flips through several more pictures:*) Sweetie?

(**MARA** *emerges from the bathroom.*)

Mara.

MARA. What?

CARTER. What is this?

MARA. Let me see.

(*Re: The picture:*) That's a child.

(**CARTER** *flips through more pictures.*)

CARTER. Lots of them.

MARA. Look at that smile.

CARTER. Yeah.

MARA. Isn't he gorgeous?

CARTER. These are from the temple?

MARA. Some. Most of those are from the Foundation.

CARTER. The what?

MARA. The Cambodian Care Foundation.

CARTER. The Cambodian…

MARA. It's a place for children.

CARTER. I see that. I thought Sopoan took you to a Wat.

MARA. He did. Then he took me to the Cambodian Care Foundation.

CARTER. Why would he do that?

MARA. I don't know. I think Dr. Heng asked him to.

CARTER. He did?

MARA. He did. Dr. Heng founded it or something. They provide care for one hundred and seventy children. Their official capacity is one hundred and fifteen but I have a feeling that Dr. Heng doesn't like to say no.

CARTER. So it's a hospital or a…like an orphanage type place?

MARA. Did you know that the adult life expectancy in this particular area is forty-nine?

CARTER. Mara –

MARA. Malaria, dengue, AIDS, landmines –

CARTER. Mara, look at me.

MARA. You should see how they care for each other. The children I mean. They have no one to belong to, so they belong to each other.

CARTER. That's nice.

MARA. No. It's not. It's the most awful, aching, horrible –

CARTER. Mara –

MARA. Every single one of them is –

CARTER. Sweetie –

MARA. Don't. Don't tell me I'm being unreasonable or that I'm reacting to some temporary pain that –

CARTER. *(Into phone:)* Brian I'm… Yup. Yeah, uh. I met with him today. Can I call you back on this? Can – uh huh… Which paper? No… No, I haven't read it –

MARA. I'm not going to talk to you about the suffering of children. You'll say something about the world being the world. You'll dismiss it.

CARTER. *(Into phone:)* Because I was meeting with him. Yes, all day. What do you think I – Look I have to call you back. Brian –

MARA. But you won't dismiss me. Because you know that you are unequipped. You are unequipped to suffer like I –

CARTER. *(To* **MARA***:)* That's unfair.

MARA. Is it?

CARTER. Stop.

MARA. You try to imagine it. I know you do.

CARTER. *(Into phone:)* Brian, I have to –

MARA. I know you believe you would take this from me if you could. I know you say that to yourself.
(Choking up:) But you can't…

(**CARTER** *hangs up the phone.* **MARA** *fights for composure. He reaches for her. She pulls away.*)

MARA. You can't. You know you can't… And I know why you brought me here.

CARTER. Mara –

MARA. Because it's Christmas. And you didn't want me to be alone. With the mail. With the cards. From our friends. Your colleagues. And their children–

CARTER. That's not why I –

MARA. It is. You know it is. Because I put them on the refrigerator. I leave them up there for months. I leave them for longer than anyone else would. To prove to you that I can still take it.

CARTER. Okay, I'm going to bring you home.

MARA. And I get hungry. And I go to the refrigerator and I stare at their perfect little faces. I mean, it's a God-damned miracle I don't starve, don't you think?

CARTER. Listen. We'll go home. We'll call the agency again.

MARA. No! No. They won't help us.

CARTER. They were optimistic. We should be opti –

MARA. Wake up baby. When you lose one, they don't give you another.

(**CARTER**'s *phone begins to ring. He looks at it.*)

CARTER. We're going to talk about this. We're not done here, all right? We're going to talk.

MARA. *(Showing him a picture:)* He has green eyes. What are the chances?

CARTER. I have to take this.

MARA. Look at him.

CARTER. No.

MARA. Look.

CARTER. Stop.

MARA. A nation of black-eyed people. Except for one. And he came to me. And his hair sticks up in the back like...

(**CARTER.** *answers the phone. He retrieves the newspaper from the table.*)

CARTER. *(Into phone:)* Yup. I'm here. What page?

MARA. He came to me. And I said it.

CARTER. *(Into phone:)* No. Of course I didn't hang – the connection.

MARA. I said it without thinking.

CARTER. *(Into phone:)* I am looking at it now Brian. I am trying to... Slow down – It says, what? For what? Could you – Hello?

MARA. Like it was a fact. I said the name. And he smiled.

CARTER. *(Into phone:)* No, it's only a problem if... I'll ask. I'll find out... I'm sure there's a perfectly good – Right. No. I'll fix it. Right. I've got this Brian. That's right. No. No. I'm here.

(Blackout.)

(The Villa. Mid-day. The remnants of a large meal and several empty bottles of wine sit on the table where **MARA**, **ROM CHANG**, **CARTER**, *and* **DR. HENG** *are seated.)*

CARTER. Look, it's a global marketplace. Let's say we have a worker. He's in, I don't know, Oklahoma. Wherever. Let's call him Bob.

ROM CHANG. Bob.

CARTER. Bob. Bob is American. And he is expensive. Bob probably belongs to a union for God's sake.

ROM CHANG. This is good for Bob.

CARTER. No. Bad. It's bad for Bob.

MARA. That's a matter of opinion. It's something we Americans debate.

CARTER. Right. We debate it, but it's bad.

ROM CHANG. Bad?

CARTER. Bob's union wants Bob to have all sorts of expensive things. Bob's union wants me, Bob's employer, to pay for these expensive things. You understand?

ROM CHANG. Bob cannot have expensive things.

HENG. I believe Carter's view is that Bob does not need expensive things.

CARTER. That's right.

ROM CHANG. Carter will share his things with Bob.

HENG. No. No my dear, he will not.

ROM CHANG. They will form a collective –

CARTER. No. Okay – Let's just back up. Look, I send Bob's job to India. Because he's expensive. So I give Bob's job to Joe. So, Joe in India does Bob's job for much less than Bob. Joe, now has a good job. And I take the money I save with Joe and I pass that savings on to my consumers. And everybody wins.

MARA. Except for Bob.

CARTER. Okay, devil's advocate. Yes. And I knew you were going to say that. So look, I just made things less expensive for Bob. And less expensive for my company. Which helps Bob's economy. So, Bob now has a good economy and some extra money that he will use to re-train. Bob will get a new job.

ROM CHANG. What will Bob do?

CARTER. It doesn't matter.

MARA. It matters to Bob.

CARTER. Bob has freedom Sweetie. Bob can do whatever he wants.

ROM CHANG. Perhaps he will be a farmer.

CARTER. Sure. There you go. A farmer. Why not.

ROM CHANG. And in the day, he will work the earth with his hands. At night, he will crouch by the fire with his comrades in Oklahoma and read from The Little Red Book of Mao Tze Tung.

CARTER. You haven't spent much time in Oklahoma.

ROM CHANG. And he will come into your house when you sleep. And let the blood from your neck with the blade of his axe. And then Bob will do your job. Because you have made it his purpose.

(An awkward pause. Then **HENG** *starts to laugh.* **CARTER** *joins in.)*

HENG. You will add that to your presentation Carter!

CARTER. I'll put it in the Powerpoint! I'll make a slide!

*(***HENG** *and* **CARTER** *laugh some more.)*

HENG. *(Raising his glass:)* I toast to the partnership between a great company and a great people. May our endeavor bring prosperity to both.

(They toast.)

CARTER. I don't like to make guarantees Dr. Heng, but trust me, this is going to be revolutionary.

HENG. *(To* **ROM CHANG***:)* Do you hear? He speaks of revolution.

ROM CHANG. I hear.

*(They all laugh except for **MARA**. **SOPOAN** enters from outside.)*

CARTER. Sopoan!

SOPOAN. The van is ready Mr. Carter.

CARTER. Great. We're just finishing up here. Hey, Mara tells me you're quite the picture taker.

*(No response. **SOPOAN** looks to **HENG**. A beat.)*

ROM CHANG. Eng prap koat tha mech? *[What did you say to him?]*

CARTER. I was thinking maybe you could take some pictures of the site. You know, so I can show the folks back home.

SOPOAN. Of course, Mr. Carter.

CARTER. Great. I brought the Nikon. You know how to work a digital?

SOPOAN. Do you have Polaroid?

CARTER. I do not have the Polaroid.

SOPOAN. Polaroid is better.

CARTER. Is that so? Why is that Sopoan?

MARA. Carter.

SOPOAN. Oh yes. With Polaroid, you take picture. And then you are waiting…and you are waiting…

CARTER. And –

SOPOAN. And you begin to see. This moment. These faces in the gray. They come toward you. They come toward you like a – how do you say?

*(To **HENG** and **ROM CHANG**:)*

Kmaow.

HENG. Ghosts.

SOPOAN. Like ghosts. Yes. It takes time. And you remember this moment but, it is different now in Polaroid. Something changed. While you were waiting. The picture changed. Or maybe you change. In the time that pass. And what you thought you saw, you did not see.

(A beat.)

CARTER. Can I attach it to an email?

SOPOAN. No Mr. Carter.

CARTER. We may have to settle for digital.

*(**SOPOAN** gives a little bow and heads for the door.)*

I appreciate it buddy. I'll see if we can get you a little cash, you know, for the expertise.

SOPOAN I will get the van.

*(**SOPOAN** gives a little bow and exits.)*

HENG. You are very kind to Sopoan.

CARTER. He's my buddy. What can I say, we hit it off.

ROM CHANG. What is "buddy"?

CARTER. Buddy. It means friend.

ROM CHANG. I thought perhaps it means pet.

CARTER. Excuse me?

HENG. Carter, I know you will find the site to your liking. I have arranged a small ceremony for the signing of the lease agreement, here, the day after tomorrow.
(Beat.) Carter?

CARTER. *(To **ROM CHANG**.)* It means friend.

HENG. Carter?

CARTER. Yes sir.

HENG. You will sign the lease with the minister, here, in two days.

CARTER. Thank you sir. Well, I suppose we should…

HENG. Yes. Please, let me walk you out.

*(**HENG** rises and begins to escort **CARTER** to the door.)*

CARTER. *(To **MARA**:)* Are you coming?

MARA. Oh. Did you want me to?

CARTER. Well I thought you'd like to see it.

MARA. There's something to see?

CARTER. It's the site.

MARA. No. I know. But I mean, it's just a field somewhere, right?

CARTER. Well it's a field now but… Come on, get your things.

MARA. Sopoan was going to take me to Angkor Thom tomorrow and I just wanted to ask Dr. Heng about –

CARTER. I really don't think we should bother Dr. Heng sweetie.

HENG. It's no trouble at all.

CARTER. Yes, but I'm sure that we don't want to overstay our welcome –

MARA. It's just a few questions Carter.

HENG. It will be my honor to discuss my country's treasures with your wife.

CARTER. Well, Sopoan is our ride back and I –

HENG. I will arrange for Mara to return to the hotel.

(Beat.)

CARTER. Excellent.

HENG. Of course. Now you must go Carter. It is late and the site is quite some distance from Phnom Penh. We do not want you wandering in the dark.

CARTER. No, we don't want that.

*(**CARTER** begins to leave. He stops.)*

MARA. I'll see you back at the hotel.

*(**HENG** leads **CARTER** out the door.)*

ROM CHANG. You would like wine?

MARA. No.

ROM CHANG. You would like tea?

MARA. No. Thank you. If you don't mind me asking, what exactly does your husband do?

ROM CHANG. Your husband did not tell you this?

MARA. I'm not sure he explained…completely.

ROM CHANG. Dr. Heng is a facilitator of course.

MARA. Facilitator.

ROM CHANG. Perhaps your corporation wishes to build a hotel in Siem Reap to contain many Chinese tourists. You will require government permits for this. Dr. Heng will get these for you.

MARA. I see.

ROM CHANG. My husband help many people Mara. He help small people. Big people. He help foreign people. He help government people. These people are grateful to my husband. Perhaps someday, he will help you too.

MARA. But I don't want anything.

(**ROM CHANG** *begins to exit.*)

No. Wait… Please. I…

ROM CHANG. You want tea?

MARA. No. I just wanted to ask you about… The other day…

ROM CHANG. Yes?

(*A beat.* **ROM CHANG** *begins to approach* **MARA**.)

MARA. When we were here – when you…you held my hand and –

ROM CHANG. *(Reaching:)* You have pain?

(**MARA.** *pulls her hand away as if from a flame.*)

MARA. No… No. I don't have pain. Not anymore.

ROM CHANG. This is good.

MARA. But I did. And it was…

ROM CHANG. *(Re:* **MARA**'s *shoulder:)* Here.

MARA. Yes.

ROM CHANG. And now?

(*Pause.*)

MARA. What did you do?

ROM CHANG. You are welcome.

(**ROM CHANG** *begins to exit.*)

MARA. No. Wait –

ROM CHANG. I must get tea.

MARA. Would you please just – Look, I said don't want any tea.

(ROM CHANG. turns to her. A beat.)

ROM CHANG. Imagine if you can, that the tea is not for you.

(ROM CHANG. exits.)

(A beat. **MARA.** *stands. She sits. She produces a newspaper from her bag. She puts it back. Short pause. She hears* **HENG.** *from outside.)*

HENG. *(Entering:)* You would have no way of knowing how rare is such a night in Phnom Penh. We have only three seasons here. The hot. The wet. And the very hot and very wet. But tonight, I believe the heavens do conspire on your behalf.

MARA. I must have friends in high places.

HENG. You do now. Would you like some tea?

MARA. I think it's already on it's way.

HENG. My wife is too good to me. She brings me what I want before I know I want it.

MARA. How nice.

HENG. It is a valuable skill to anticipate another's need. Don't you agree?

(Beat.)

Mara?

(No response.)

Are you all right?

MARA. Yes.

(Short pause.)

HENG. You have no reason to be anxious.

MARA. I'm not.

HENG. But you are perhaps being untruthful.

MARA. I'm not anxious.

HENG. Yes. But you are shaking.

(HENG. reaches out and takes MARA's hands. A beat. She pulls them away.)

MARA. I just – I haven't been sleeping well and I –

HENG. It is natural to have anxiety in a strange place. After all, even reasonable people know there is always madness and death somewhere beyond the door. In Cambodia. In Brooklyn.

MARA. What?

HENG. I have said something to upset you?

(Beat.)

MARA. Bad things happen everywhere Dr. Heng.

HENG. Yes.

MARA. People do bad things.

HENG. Yes they do.

MARA. And they… There is…justice.

(Beat.)

HENG. Is there? And who will be your judge?

MARA. What?

(Beat.)

HENG. Mara… It is not true.

MARA. I don't know what you –

HENG. Look at me.

(She does.)

HENG. It is, not true.

(Short pause.)

MARA. There were children there?

HENG. You cannot understand.

(Pause. MARA reaches into her bag and takes out the newspaper.)

MARA. It says that they took the children into the courtyard and beat their heads against the trees.

HENG. You do not understand.

MARA. To save *bullets*?

(**HENG** *looks away. Short pause.*)

How many did they save?

HENG. No one was saved.

MARA. How many *bullets* did they save?

HENG. You don't understand.

MARA. How many?

(*No response. A beat.*)

MARA. (*Reads:*) The Extraordinary Chambers of the Courts of Cambodia will convene this week for the first of several fact-finding sessions –

HENG. International Tribune?

MARA. The panel will hear evidence and decide whether to add to the six suspected Khmer Rouge figures currently awaiting trial on charges including genocide and crimes against humanity.

HENG. It's quite ironic –

MARA. The first of these hearings is expected to focus on former Interior Minister Dr. Son Heng who currently resides at his villa in Phnom Penh.

HENG. Ah, it's a villa now.

MARA. UN appointed prosecution lawyers from several western nations will provide evidence in an effort to prove that Heng is in fact, "The Doctor". A notorious figure said to have administrated the –

HENG. – prison and interrogation center that existed at the People's Hospital in Kampong Trabek from 1975 to 1978. It is actually shameful –

(*Crossing to her:*)

HENG.	**MARA.**
– how much they diminish me. Of course they leave out is that I was in charge of the entire province –	(*Reads:*) It was previously thought that none of the over sixteen thousand Cambodians interrogated at Kampong survived. However –

(**HENG** *snatches the paper from* **MARA***'s hand.*)

HENG. That's enough! You shouldn't… That's enough.

MARA. They have a witness.

HENG. They have a farce. They have ghost stories to present for your media and notions of moral superiority. But of course you believe what you read. Not what you see. Not whom you know –

MARA. It says there that you are this Doctor.

HENG. I am a doctor of economics! I am a facilitator. And I made money, yes. And I have made enemies, yes. But this is not a crime. This so-called hearing is nothing more than an attempt by my competitors to exploit the ignorance of the United Nations. To embarrass me. To steal my clients.

(**HENG** *goes to pour more wine.*)

This Doctor – This person does not even exist. This is a figment. This is a story we told to peasants to keep them in the fields.

MARA. You admit you were involved.

HENG. The war lasted twenty-three years. Two million people died. You're asking if I was involved?

MARA. You were Khmer Rouge.

HENG. (*Building, with force:*) You say Khmer Rouge as if it were a faction. It was not. It was a time. Who was Khmer Rouge? Was I Khmer Rouge? Yes, I was Khmer Rouge. The men outside were Khmer Rouge. Our Prime Minister, Hun Sen himself, was Khmer Rouge. Do you know how to tell if someone in Cambodia was Khmer Rouge? Do you?

MARA. No.

HENG. You can tell, because they are alive.

(**MARA** *watches as* **HENG** *goes to the window. He looks out and finishes his wine. He pours more. Pause.*)

Go home Mara. Go back to your doorman.

(**MARA** *does not move. Pause.*)

HENG. *(Cont.)* You read these rumors in the paper. You gawk at me like I am some monster. But you do not go.

(MARA doesn't move. Long pause. Still facing the window, HENG begins to tremble. His wine spills. He tries to brace himself on the window.)

Why are you still here?

MARA. I…

HENG. Do you even know?

MARA. I wanted…

(Short pause. HENG produces a folder from a drawer. A Polaroid is clipped to the front.)

Is this it? Is this what you need?

(ROM CHANG enters.)

ROM CHANG. No.

(She slams the tea-set down and tries to wrest the folder from HENG.)

HENG. His name is Somnang. He is –

ROM CHANG. Stop! Stop it! Do not bow to these people.

HENG. Shh…

ROM CHANG. Mon amour non, Ils nous detestest. *[My love, no. They hate us.]*

HENG. There are no choices. There is no time.

ROM CHANG. Je mourais plutot. Je mourais plutot avec toi. *[I would rather die. I would rather die with you.]*

HENG. *(To MARA:)* His name is Somnang. He is twenty-two months old.

(Extending the folder to MARA:)

This is the one, yes?

(Beat.)

Go on. Take it.

(She does. MARA touches the picture.)

MARA. Somnang.

HENG. It means "fortunate".

MARA. Somnang.

(HENG clings to ROM CHANG. Their foreheads touching.)

ROM CHANG. Je reste. Je resterai avec toi. *[I stay. I stay with you.]*

HENG. *(To ROM CHANG:)* They will come for me. At night. They will have dogs.

MARA. How much?

HENG. They will speak their lies until they are true.

ROM CHANG. No.

HENG. *(To ROM CHANG:)* And then they will come for you.

ROM CHANG. Let them come.

HENG. I cannot. You know I cannot.

(HENG holds ROM CHANG as if for the last time. She clings to him as he looks to MARA.)

MARA. How much?

HENG. Yes. Isn't that the way of you people. To tolerate us only so long as we are useful.

(Blackout.)

(Contained light up on **SOPOAN**. *He sits in a wooden chair.)*

SOPOAN. When I awake. There was no sound. Nothing. Not even the termite. The hole was closed. So I dig. And I come up through the earth like a dead man who is not dead. I remember, there is quiet. I remember, there is soft rain on my skin. I remember, there is a smell.

(Short pause.)

I could not see very much. Only shape. Only light. I call her name many times. I call, Chantrea? Chantrea? **Chantrea, neak nau te?** *[Are you there Chantrea?]* Like that. But there is nothing. I feel to the door of our home. But there is no one in my home. There is no one in my neighbor home. And it was hard to breathe. And I could not see. But I begin to run. I run all through the streets of my district. I am calling her name. But I hear only my own voice, laughing at me from the walls. And I am running. And I cannot see. And I fall into the canal. And there is a man in the canal. And there many other people with him. In the canal. And I am in the canal. And I am looking for my wife and I cannot see, but with my hands. I begin...

(Pause.)

...to feel their faces. All of them. Man face. Woman face. Old face. Young face. Children face. And I am floating in the water. And there is blood in the water. And bodies in the water. And I knew them... This is where they found me. The Khmer Rouge.

(Pause.) I did not see her face again for a long time.

(Blackout.)

End of Act I

ACT II

(Contained light up on **SOPOAN**. *He sits in a wooden chair.)*

SOPOAN. When I come to the fields. I ask many people if they had saw my wife. A man I knew from our temple said she was on the truck that went to Phumi Dei Lo. A soldier say that he shot her on Street 556. But I did not believe him because he was a teenager and they like to make up stories like that. It was hard to ask questions because our talking was forbidden. And color was forbidden. We got black clothes.

(Short pause.)

And to rest was forbidden. And to look at CPK soldiers was forbidden. And to have religion was forbidden. And to call person by their old name was forbidden. We do work in the fields to help make our minds like revolutionary mind. To know our crimes. Do you understand?

(Short pause.)

I am in the field three years. It is very hard to think about revolution all of the time. I mostly think about my wife then. Maybe where she was. If she was alive. We have one bowl of rice each day. We work eighteen hour. So I think many people dream about food most of the time. When you are in the field, you cannot think about things you do not have. If you think about food you do not have, then you will lose your revolutionary enthusiasm. CPK soldier will see that you are doing economic sabotage and he will put you on the truck.

(Beat.)

After some time, I did no more thinking about my wife. I think only of the earth. And how it is old. And how it is green. And how it will be green when we are gone. And sometimes, I paint pictures in my head.

(Blackout.)

*(The Villa. **MARA** and **CARTER** sit across from **ROM CHANG** and **HENG**. **HENG** holds the folder with the Polaroid clipped to its front.)*

HENG. Somnang is twenty-two months old. Of course, it is impossible to be entirely accurate in these circumstances.

MARA. Of course.

CARTER. Som…

ROM CHANG. *(Helping him pronounce it:)* Som-nang.

CARTER. Som-nang. Close?

ROM CHANG. For you. Yes.

CARTER. *(Trying it out:)* Somnang.

HENG. Flawless, Carter. Very good.

MARA. It means, fortunate.

HENG. I think we all agree this boy could not have a more appropriate name. Though I imagine you could change this if –

MARA. No. No, that won't be necessary.

HENG. You know what is best. This second page details his medical history. I am afraid there was no time for translation.

MARA. Is he…

HENG. He is fine Mara. Perfectly healthy. Some fever, some intestinal problems when he was very young but I am told this is normal.

MARA. It is.

HENG. There was some observation done by…

(Scanning the contents:) Ah, yes. Somnang is very intelligent. He sleeps well. He eats well. This is all very good.

*(**HENG** flips a few more pages. He closes the folder. He removes the Polaroid from the cover.)*

CARTER. Um… Dr. Heng.

HENG. Yes Carter.

CARTER. I just wanted to… I mean, before we get ahead of ourselves here –

HENG. Is there a problem?

MARA. No. There's no problem.

CARTER. May I ask Dr. Heng a question?

HENG. Please.

CARTER. It's just that this is all happening rather fast for us and –

HENG. I understand.

CARTER. Believe me, I don't want to seem ungrateful.

MARA. We are very grateful.

CARTER. But. Well, if you had any idea what we've been through with – having children. I mean you think that it's some automatic biological right but…

MARA. Carter.

CARTER. We've been through a lot, Dr. Heng. My wife has.

HENG. I understand the cruelty of such a circumstance.

CARTER. So I just want to be sure that we understand each other. And that no one's expectations are…unrealistic or –

ROM CHANG. You do not trust us?

MARA. That's not what he's saying.

ROM CHANG. You do not want this child?

CARTER. No. Look, I'm not saying – Look. This all just happening very fast, all right. And under the circumstances, I think I'd prefer to go through the usual channels here.

HENG. I am the usual channels here.

CARTER. I know. But I would maybe feel a little more comfortable if we had some official structure or agency or document that –

HENG. I see.

CARTER. It's not about trust. It's just –

HENG. Business.

CARTER. Yes.

HENG. I explained to your wife why it is necessary to proceed in this manner. You must understand that a couple like you is not permitted to adopt a child here in Cambodia.

CARTER. See I don't understand that. That doesn't seem –

(**MARA** *places her hand on* **CARTER.**)

HENG. Of course we would not deny our orphans a home. But I am afraid that your American State Department forbids you to bring a Cambodian child to your country.

CARTER. Is that so?

HENG. They claim that by eliminating this demand, they will stop the unfortunate practice of selling children. And so they punish precisely those they wish to protect. However, while an American woman cannot bring a Cambodian child to the United States –

MARA. A Cambodian woman can.

(*Pause.* **CARTER** *looks to* **ROM CHANG.**)

CARTER. Right. And what would something like this...cost.

MARA. No.

HENG. Why do you insult us?

MARA. I'm sorry. He's sorry.

HENG. We are talking about a human being. A child. There can be no price for this.

CARTER. I apologize.

ROM CHANG. I forgive you.

HENG. Rom Chang has offered to help you in this matter. She will require a sponsor for her visa. I presume PanaTel could arrange some sort of temporary...

CARTER. Right. I can look into it.

MARA. Look into it?

CARTER. I'll talk to Brian, okay?

HENG. Very good. And they will accommodate Rom Chang throughout the adoption proceeding there. And you Carter. You will look after my wife… It is as if you hold my beating heart in your hands. I trust you with this. Do you understand?

CARTER. Yes.

HENG. I know he will be a fine boy. And you will be exceptional parents. Because of your generosity, this child will know prosperity and opportunity that he otherwise –

(**HENG** *stops when he notices* **SOPOAN** *has entered.*)

SOPOAN. Excuse. The van is ready Miss Mara.

MARA. I'll be right there.

CARTER. Where are you going?

MARA. I told you, Dr. Heng arranged a visit.

CARTER. What, now?

MARA. Yes.

CARTER. You're going to visit the…

MARA. Somnang.

CARTER. I know his name.

MARA. This is how it's done here. It's better this way. It's simple this way.

CARTER. Can we just talk about this please?

MARA. We are.

CARTER. I mean, in private.

HENG. *(Re: the picture.)* You know, it is remarkable.

MARA. What is?

HENG. Well the boy is Khmer but…

(*Showing the picture to* **MARA** *and* **CARTER**:) Do you see?

CARTER. What?

HENG. I dare say, there is a resemblance. Do you agree?

MARA. Yes. Yes I do.

CARTER. Resemblance?

MARA. Yes.

(MARA goes to him. She touches his face.)

Do you know what this is?

CARTER. Mara –

MARA. This is grace Carter. It's grace.

(Beat.)

Do you see?

CARTER. I see.

MARA. This is grace.

(She kisses him.)

(To **SOPOAN***:)* Are you ready?

SOPOAN. Yes Miss Mara.

*(***SOPOAN** *escorts* **MARA** *out.* **HENG** *crosses and pours wine from the decanter. A beat.)*

HENG. *(Bringing* **CARTER** *a glass:)* The Buddhists say that merit accumulates. I believe we have all added to our coffers here today.

CARTER. What are you doing?

HENG. I am making a toast.

CARTER. You're manipulating my wife.

HENG. I beg your pardon.

CARTER. And I don't appreciate it –

HENG. You misunderstand –

CARTER. No. No I do not misunderstand. I see exactly what you're doing here.

ROM CHANG. You do not speak to my husband like this.

CARTER. Yes I do. Because you are way out of line sir. Do you hear me? This is business. You do not involve my wife – you don't – You do not take a person, a vulnerable person and exploit –

ROM CHANG. Kwat nih chilouey nas – *[This man has no respect –]*

CARTER. And don't do that –

ROM CHANG. Net mun mian chet sah –

CARTER. Don't do that. Stop that God dammit. If you want to say something, say it to my face.

ROM CHANG. *(To his face:)* **Net mun mian chet sah.**

CARTER. Oh that's great. What did she say? Go on. Tell me what you said.

(Beat.)

HENG. My wife said that your heart is cold.

(A beat.)

CARTER. My... You know nothing about my heart.

ROM CHANG. I know you are ungrateful for this gift we give you.

CARTER. Oh it's a gift? Right. That's what this is. And it has nothing to do with getting someone's wife out of the country, right? This has nothing to do with a hearing. A hearing that's obviously going to become a trial, that –

ROM CHANG. My husband is innocent!

CARTER. *(Overlapping:)* Bullshit! Bullshit!

ROM CHANG. **Net mun dang ai sah Am ri kang!** *[You know nothing American!]*

HENG. *(Overlapping:)* **Chenh tou!** *[Leave us.]*

ROM CHANG. **Net mun dang ai sah!**

HENG. **Chou!** *[Stop!]*

ROM CHANG. You think you know what is happening here? You want to give me economic lecture? I say to you ten million.

CARTER. What?

ROM CHANG. This is the number of people in Cambodia. And this is also the number of landmine.

HENG. My dear please –

ROM CHANG. And if you were to dig Carter Dean – And you would have to do this most careful because they are quite old, but you would find instruction painted on landmine. In Chinese, in Russian, in Czech, in English –

CARTER. I don't have to listen to this –

ROM CHANG. And now, thirty years later, United Nations spends 120 million dollars to put on trial six old men in a country where our people make less than fifty cent a day. And you think my husband is behaving like the guilty one?

HENG. Rom Chang.

ROM CHANG. And what if he is? If my husband and six old men are guilty, are all of you innocent? Is it resolved?

CARTER. *(Rising:)* I'm going to go.

ROM CHANG. Is it resolved so you can build your call center here. Build luxury hotel. Build your golf courses on our graves?

HENG. Carter wait.

ROM CHANG. Let him go.

HENG. *(To* **ROM CHANG***:)* Leave us.

ROM CHANG. Are we clean for you then?

*(***ROM CHANG** *exits.)*

Forgive her. She is only frightened.

(Short pause.)

The first time I saw my wife, she was standing in a courtyard. I cannot describe for you the madness of that place and time. But I remember her. And I remember all the others around her. The gray skin. Swollen stomachs. Empty cheeks, empty eyes, all of them. Except for this solitary girl. And she seemed… entirely untouched…and I knew.

I knew I was looking at the last unbroken thing in all the world. And I reached out my hand. And she looked at me. And I knew love existed. Even in that courtyard. Even in me. Do you know what that is to feel?

*(***CARTER** *looks at* **HENG***. A beat.)*

CARTER. Yes.

HENG. We are not so different. And I see now that you are not like the others. I can give Brian every assurance that nothing will come of this hearing. And he asks only that your company be spared awkward publicity. He never asks if I am or I am not this Doctor.

CARTER. Are you?

HENG. There is no such person, you must understand.

CARTER. I understand, that asking me to take your wife out of Cambodia is the act of a very frightened, very guilty man.

HENG. That word again.

CARTER. That's right.

HENG. Well, certainly someone must be. Of course, in matters such as this, I find there are always differing accounts. Each one told in the language of its own madness. Each one full of subtle distinctions and meanings that will be lost on you who were not here. The United Nations will make records of these nightmares. They will select the common elements and call that the truth. I know what this trial is Carter. I have seen the mechanism at work. And I know it will not reason. It will not feel.

(Building, with force:)

It will only proceed. And consume. And if you believe that I am frightened for myself then you have never loved anything in your life. I say let them come for me. But I will not watch them drag that innocent flower into the street –

(Choking up:)

to tear her apart. Or worse. To shun her…to just leave her alone to… What would you do?

(Composes himself, a beat.)

And I was afraid, yes. But now I am not.

Because you are here. And we are each other's answer. What was it your wife called it? Grace.

CARTER. I can't help you.

HENG. You will. And you will help yourself. Your company, your career, your wife –

CARTER. No. It stops here. You have no right to reach into our lives, our personal lives. This is business.

HENG. I am very sorry, but we have never had the luxury of that distinction here.

CARTER. You're going to tell Mara it fell through. Do you understand?

HENG. You will take Rom Chang or the ministry will not approve your project. Do you understand?

CARTER. You tell her it fell through.

HENG. Your wife wants this child very much Carter... I find it strange that you do not feel the same.

(**CARTER** *heads for the door.*)

(*Beat.*)

What happened to the child? The one you lost.

CARTER. What?

HENG. We know very well the kind of woman who does not speak of her children.

CARTER. You should shut your mouth.

(**SOPOAN** *enters.*)

HENG. We have many of these women here. I think you will find there is nothing weak about their sex.

Our revolution proved that they are the ones who have the capacity to act. To see clearly what is necessary and to do it. Did you know that a man chained to iron rail will stare at bowl of rice just out of his reach until he starves. But that very first night Carter, the woman sets to work on her wrist.

SOPOAN. Mr. Carter will return to the hotel now?

(*Beat.*)

Mr. Carter?

(**SOPOAN** *opens the door.* **CARTER** *heads out.*)

HENG. I know something of love and human nature. Believe me, you will be surprised by what you do.

SOPOAN. Mr. Carter?

CARTER. Let's go.

*(**CARTER** exits.)*

*(**SOPOAN** looks to **HENG**.)*

HENG. Tell the woman, there isn't much time.

*(**SOPOAN** exits. **HENG** sits into his chair. He drinks.)*

(Blackout.)

*(Lights up on **SOPOAN**. He sits in a wooden chair.)*

SOPOAN. Sopoan is dead. Sopoan is in the hospital now. Sopoan is in the hands of Khmer Rouge now. Khmer Rouge will never let Sopoan go. I believe them when they say this.

(Beat.)

So I stopped to be Sopoan.

(Beat.)

To live, the prisoner must change. To escape, the prisoner becomes something new. I became Sopoan, a man who could do magic things.

(Beat.)

The Khmer Rouge chain me to iron rail. But I turn iron rail into Monivong, the river of my youth. The cuff on my wrist, I make the hand of my wife.
The stain on the wall, was my window... And I could see her.

(Beat.)

That is not a wire, it is a feather. That is not a razor, it is a violin. You are not a soldier, you are my father. That is not blood in the dirt. That is rice.

*(Blackout. Lights up on the Hotel Room. **MARA** is banging on the bathroom door.)*

MARA. Carter?. Carter, what the hell happened? Will you open this door please. Carter!

(Beat.)

Sweetie?

(Beat.)

Look, Sopoan said some... He had some very confusing things to say in the van and I just...well I'm confused. Who are you talking to? Carter, open this door.

(Beat.) And I know you're probably confused...we need to be thinking clearly here Carter. Sweetie, open this fucking door right now.

(Rattling the door:)

I'm your wife.

*(**CARTER** exits the bathroom. A beat.)*

MARA. Was that... Were you talking to Brian?
CARTER. Yes.

(Beat.)

MARA. What did you tell him?
CARTER. It doesn't matter.
MARA. Of course it does. Carter, talk to me.
CARTER. I think I woke him up...it's kind of late there.

(Looks at his watch. Beat.)

Merry Christmas by the way.

MARA. What did he say?
CARTER. Nothing.
MARA. Nothing?
CARTER. I hung up.
MARA. Why would you –
CARTER. Would you please just let me think for a second.

(Pause.)

He's guilty.

*(They sit is silence for a moment. Then **CARTER** retrieves a suitcase and begins to pack.)*

MARA. What are you doing?

CARTER. We never should have come.

*(**CARTER** starts to pack their things.)*

MARA. Wait. Wait.

CARTER. They're using us.

MARA. Can we talk about this please?

CARTER. *(Packing:)* We do this. I mean, this is what we do, isn't it? We do this all the time.

MARA. Listen to me –

CARTER. We walk into a place like this. We act like we have answers. Like we're going to give them something, right? As if we know what they need. And we don't. We don't know anything. Barely anything. We know just enough to fuck it all up.

(She blocks his way.)

CARTER. *(Moving around her:)* Excuse me.

MARA. We can't go.

CARTER. We don't have a choice. Do you get it? I don't care what he says. This isn't politics or – They're going to indict this man. We cannot be here. We're not getting involved with something like this.

(He heads into the bathroom.)

MARA. We are involved Carter. We are here. We are here now. Carter?

*(**CARTER** comes out of the bathroom with his shaving kit, her cosmetics.)*

MARA. *(Blocking him:)* Stop it. Stop.

CARTER. What are you doing?

MARA. Look at me.

CARTER. This isn't a negotiation.

(**CARTER** *moves around her, continues packing.*)

MARA. What about these people?

CARTER. Get your things Mara.

MARA. What about Somnang? What about Rom Chang?

CARTER. Mara. Please.

(*Beat. Checks his watch:*)

I think there's a six o'clock flight… Mara.

(*No response.* **CARTER** *crosses to her.*)

This is thirty years of murder and torture and – God knows what. And that man is involved. He is responsible. You know he is. We can't interfere with –

MARA. We have a deal.

CARTER. Sweetie…

(*He takes her in his arms. She puts her head on his chest.*)

MARA. We have a deal.

CARTER. No. There's no deal.

MARA. Yes there is. Because we are still owed something here Carter.

(*Welling up:*) I am owed. God dammit, I am owed…

CARTER. I know… I'm sorry… It just has to wait.

MARA. Wait?

(*Breaking away from him:*)

Wait? I'm a mother without a child. What is that?

CARTER. Don't do this Sweetie. Please.

MARA. We… We can go get Rom Chang now. And then we can go to the –

CARTER. Stop.

MARA. We'll pick up Somnang and –

CARTER. Stop it.

MARA. We had a deal.

CARTER. The man is a God damn war criminal!

MARA. I don't care.

(Short pause. Off **CARTER**:*)*

Don't look at me like that.

CARTER. Jesus Christ. I am talking about human beings.

MARA. So am I.

(Short pause. **CARTER** *starts packing again. Short pause.)*

MARA. What does it matter what happened? Carter... Those people are dead.

(He looks at her and begins packing faster.)

But that Child is alive. That woman is alive. And I am alive Carter. You are alive. We survived.

CARTER. Are you listening to yourself?

MARA. If we can save these people, how is that a bad thing? How is that bad? I can't see how that's a –

CARTER. I can't talk to you when you're like this.

MARA. I'm always like this.

CARTER. I mean I am not having this conversation. I am going to forget this conversation.

MARA. Carter –

CARTER. There's nothing we can do. I cannot do what you want me to do.

MARA. Yes you can. You're the only one who can.

CARTER. Pack your things.

MARA. We can leave tomorrow.

CARTER. I can't believe you're actually willing to help this guy.

MARA. I'm helping us!

CARTER. Did you ever wonder why he wants her to get out? Did you?

MARA. It doesn't matter.

CARTER. What are you talking about? She's probably a God damned collaborator Mara. You ever think of that?

MARA. No.

CARTER. Well maybe you should.

(She watches him pack. Pause.)

MARA. *(A realization:)* You're scared.

CARTER. God damn right I am. And I can tell you one thing. I am not going to be the guy who helped the God damned Doctor and… Eva fucking Braun. Do you understand me? It is over. Do you understand? We are going home.

*(**CARTER** finishes packing. They look at each other. A beat. **MARA** watches as **CARTER** starts packing her things. Pause.)*

MARA. *(A realization:)* You don't want this child.

CARTER. Not like this.

MARA. No. You never did. Are you frightened? Is that it?

CARTER. Stop.

MARA. You're frightened.

(Short pause:)

Carter… Baby look at me.

(Beat.)

Carter…you can get on that plane with me, and with that woman, and with that child or you can…

*(**CARTER** stops packing. He stares into the suitcase. Short pause.)*

Please…don't make me say it. God damn you if you make me say it.

(A beat.)

CARTER. It didn't just happen to you.

MARA. I know that.

CARTER. And you fucking act like – like you're the only casualty here.

MARA. I know. I'm sorry. I –

CARTER. Like I wasn't obliterated. As if I wasn't – MY LIFE STOPPED!

(Beat.)

It stopped. Do you have any idea? I mean, I sit, in that fucking office. I watch it all happening without me. My life. Like I'm a ghost. I mean, it's not as if I'm going out with the guys Mara –

MARA. I know.

CARTER. I'm not getting invited to play God damn golf. No. I'm invisible. And I'm watching these guys move to the fourth floor. Guys I trained. Fucking *Brian*? Because…because I'm the sad damaged guy who's got to go home to be with the sad damaged wife and – FUCK!

*(**CARTER** sits on the bed. He's trying very hard to hold it together. **MARA** takes a step toward him.)*

*(He holds up his hand, stopping her. Then he meets her eyes. **CARTER** begins to weep.)*

MARA. This isn't something… I can live without –

CARTER. We can't replace him.

MARA. No.

CARTER. I don't want to. I don't want to replace him.

*(**CARTER** begins to fall apart. **MARA** crosses to him and takes him in her arms.)*

I just want to forget… I just want to forget him…oh my God I just want to forget…

MARA. Shhh…

CARTER. I just want to forget him…

MARA. *(Comforting him:)* No…

(A beat.)

CARTER. We never say his name.

MARA. Alex…

*(This word breaks **CARTER**.)*

CARTER. Jesus…oh my God Jesus oh my god…we don't deserve another –

MARA. Don't say that baby.

CARTER. We don't... I don't...

MARA. Shh...

(He clings to her. Pause.)

CARTER. Oh God... Just wanted to cool off. Just put my head under the water.

MARA. Stop.

CARTER. Just for a moment.

MARA. I know.

CARTER. Just looked away for a moment.

MARA. It's okay.

CARTER. Just looked away and he... and Alex... I thought you were watching.

MARA. I know.

CARTER. Why weren't you watching?

(Beat.)

MARA. I don't remember.

CARTER. No. Oh my God. I can't... I can't do this.

MARA. Yes.

CARTER. I can't.

MARA. Yes. You will.

CARTER. No.

MARA. You will. You will baby. You'll do this for me.

(He clings to her as the lights fade to black.)

*(Contained light up on **SOPOAN**. He sits in a wooden chair.)*

SOPOAN. There is a small room. There are bars on the windows. The floor is concrete. There is a chair. On the wall is many pictures of people. Old, young, soldier, monk, man, woman, like that. Many hundreds then.

(Beat.)

I am chained to the rail. We are all chained to rail there. We are all standing. We fall asleep. We hang from our arms very painful. We wake up. We are standing. We are sleeping. Hanging… Sometimes guards come. They take one person. They go away. We are standing. There is screaming. We wake up. When the person come back – The person comes back until they do not come back, do you understand? Sometimes, the person have no teeth. Sometimes, the person have no finger. Sometime, the person has no injury at all. Except that their eyes are empty and dead. This is how I know that The Doctor is real.

(Beat.)

The Khmer Rouge do many methods to help us face our treason. With electric. With needle. With plier. Everyone confess many things. You confess until you cannot imagine any more crimes you do against Angkar. Then they take you to the yard. I think it is very much like the book I read when I was a boy in the Ecole. Like Shaharazade. Do you know this story?

(Short pause:)

Sometimes, The CPK puts you on the table. Puts towel over your face. Pour water through the towel up your nose. This was the best method for helping my imagination.

(Blackout.)

*(The Villa. **ROM CHANG** stands in the center of the room facing **SOPOAN**.)*

ROM CHANG. **Ni mun mian gravuhl –** *[This is not an earing –]*
SOPOAN. English. Only English now.
ROM CHANG. This is not an earing. It is a bridge over the Monivong.

*(She hands it to **SOPOAN**. He looks at it in his hands.)*

SOPOAN. I will go there each day.
ROM CHANG. Yes. You will go.

*(**HENG** enters from downstairs with a bottle. He is drunk. He regards **SOPOAN** and **ROM CHANG** for a moment.)*

HENG. They are here.

*(**SOPOAN** heads for the front door as **ROM CHANG** exits downstairs.)*

*(**HENG** sits at the table and pours another glass of wine.)*

*(**CARTER** enters followed by **MARA** and **SOPOAN**.)*

MARA. Where is Rom Chang?
HENG. She is coming.
CARTER. *(Looking at his watch.)* Great.
MARA. Would you relax.
CARTER. We're not going to make it.
MARA. We are. Sopoan and I will go get Somnang. We'll take the van. We'll go right now.
CARTER. *(Off **MARA**:)* Okay…
Wait?

*(**HENG** watches as she kisses him.)*

MARA. *(To **CARTER**:)* Smile.
CARTER. I am smiling. See?
MARA. Okay, I'll be right back.

*(**MARA** exits with **SOPOAN**. A pause.)*

HENG. I would offer you a drink, but I am afraid this is the last of it.

CARTER. That's all right.

(A pause. **CARTER** *checks his watch.* **HENG** *drinks.)*

What exactly is Rom Chang doing?

HENG. I have no idea. Sometimes, I just have to wait.

(Beat.)

I think this may be a universal problem.

CARTER. *(Light:)* Could be.

(The men look at each other. **CARTER** *looks away. A pause.)*

HENG. It must be wonderful for you. To see your wife so happy.

CARTER. Yes. Thank you… Look I don't actually know how much time we have here so –

HENG. Carter.

CARTER. What?

HENG. You will see that my wife is happy too?

CARTER. I'll do what I said I'd do.

HENG. Yes. Good. That is good…

*(***HENG** *drinks. Short pause.)*

And you will speak to her of me sometimes?

CARTER. Dr. Heng –

HENG. Just sometimes and please…do not let her read these newspapers, these –

CARTER. Listen, I'll get her to the States, all right? But that's it. She's Brian's problem after that.

HENG. Problem?

CARTER. Responsibility. She's his responsibility.

HENG. But I asked you Carter. You gave me your word that –

CARTER. Look, I know that this is difficult for you but I can't –

HENG. I am only asking that you write to me from time to time to –

CARTER. No. No. Look that's… I can't do that, okay? And you can't communicate with me either. And not Brian – Not ever. Do you understand? I'm afraid it's just not going to be possible for us to have contact with someone like you.

(Beat.)

HENG. Someone. Like me.

CARTER. Look. I don't want to get into an argument here. I'd just like to get your wife in the car so that we all go to the airport and avoid any…complications, okay?

HENG. You still think we are so different.

CARTER. I think I'm going to wait outside.

HENG. You still do not see.

*(***CARTER.** *stops.)*

We are the same.

CARTER. Like hell we are.

HENG. But I am looking in a mirror. I see this man who cannot survive without the woman he loves. This man who would do anything now, yes? The woman needs this child to survive. The man needs this woman to survive. And he thinks, I will perform this one action – To stop her suffering. Now, is that you, or is it me there, clinging to his wife like a drowning man? We are the same.

CARTER. Except that one of us is a murderer.

HENG. Yes, I am a murderer.

CARTER. That's right.

HENG. And you are a murderer.

CARTER. You're drunk.

HENG. You are a murderer Carter. The only difference between us is that your circumstances have spared you the necessity of pulling a trigger. But believe me, you would –

CARTER. Not true –

HENG. You would. I promise you that you would –

CARTER. Bullshit –

HENG. You are a human being. The extremity of your actions is determined only by the extremity of your need.

CARTER. Rom Chang! We are leaving! We are leaving now!

HENG. So make your protestations. Tell yourself that you do this uncomfortable thing with great reluctance. Add what you do here today to the list of compromises that will make your life. But do not stand here *in my house* and pretend that you are some man and I am some monster.

CARTER. Let's get this straight. Never, not in a million years, could I do what you did in that place.

HENG. Why? Because you have morality?

CARTER. That's right.

HENG. Of course, talk about your morality Carter, and I will know you've never watched your family starve.

CARTER. I want you to know that I will be watching. When they indict you. When they try you. And when they punish you, for what you did.

HENG. What I did. I was the administrator of the hospital at Kampong Trabek.

CARTER. Rom Chang.!

HENG. And I presided. And I saw. And had it not been me, it would have been someone –

CARTER. It was you! It was, you.

HENG. Was it?

(**ROM CHANG** *enters. She is dressed to travel.*)

ROM CHANG. What is this yelling?

CARTER. We're going. Get in the Car.

HENG. It's true. I was there. And it was in that place that I learned the secret every Cambodian knows.

ROM CHANG. Qu'est que tu fais? *[What are you doing?]*

HENG. Why should this be easy for them?

ROM CHANG. Ce n'est pas le moment de punir. *[It is too late for punishment.]*

HENG. The secret Carter, is that your most tender nerves is not inside your body at all. They are hidden within the ones you love. If you wish to make a man a murderer, you do not hold a gun to his head. You hold it to his family. And this is what happened here. So do not speak to me of morality because I have seen the extremity of your wife's need. And I have seen the extremity of yours. And this is how I know with complete certainty that, to make her whole again, you would take The Doctor himself.

(A beat.)

CARTER. I'm sorry to disappoint you. But you'll be staying in Cambodia.

HENG. *(To* **CARTER***:)* The United Nations shares your opinion. And I am happy to play this part. They can have their answer. They can stop their looking. Build their hotels.

(Beat.)

But before you go, you should know that there are differing accounts, you see.

ROM CHANG. Tei.

HENG. The Khmer word for doctor is **Kruck**. This is featured in many documents and is often used to describe the administrator of Security Prison 124. Who was in fact, a Doctor of Economics.

(Beat.)

But if you were to ask the poor people. They would tell a different story. Which is unwritten and quite sensational in the way of illiterates. You see, the person they feared was not an administrator, but an interrogator from whom there was no hiding. They speak of a person who could feel your secrets through your skin. In fact, one version says that The Doctor was not a man at all. But rather, a girl who could remove any injury, and with it, memory.

(CARTER looks to ROM CHANG.)

These things are inseparable. And they called her **Kruck**, which to them means, the healer. This is a minor distinction perhaps, just a ghost story.

(MARA enters.)

MARA. Somnang is in the car. Carter, we have to go.

HENG. Vigilante is the word for the killers of killers. What do we call the victims of victims?

MARA. Please.

HENG. Victims who did what any man would do. What you will do now.

MARA. Carter…look at me.

(He does.)

HENG. And it is all you can do.

MARA. Let's go home.

(CARTER looks at his wife. He looks at ROM CHANG.)

CARTER. *(To ROM CHANG:)* Get in the car.

(ROM CHANG exits, followed by CARTER and MARA.)

(CARTER stops.)

HENG. You save what you can.

(CARTER leaves. HENG calls after him.)

Save one life Carter! Save Rom Chang! Save two. Save Somnang!

(A car engine starts. HENG follows the sound to the window, calling after it.)

Save three! Save your wife Carter! Four! Save your wife so she will save you! Save yourself! Yes! Save what you can!

(HENG slumps down into his chair. He drinks.)

(Blackout.)

*(Contained light up on **SOPOAN**. He sits in a wooden chair.)*

SOPOAN. I am on the rail six days when I meet The Doctor. I sit in chair. The Doctor know everything about me, even my name. The Doctor explain the rules for interrogation. But I do not hear them. Because I am looking at the wall. Because I see my wife picture on the wall. And this is how I know she is dead.

*(As **SOPOAN** speaks, the contained light around him slowly expands, revealing the walls and hundreds upon hundreds of 5x5 Polaroid mug shots of ordinary Cambodian people.)*

After that, I could do no more magic. I had no more stories to tell. I say to The Doctor, every accusation is true. I am a thief. I am assassin. I am KGB. I am CIA. I am anything you want me to be. And The Doctor, that man, Son Heng…he put the camera into my hands.

(Beat.)

This is how I became the photographer at Security Prison 124, at the Peoples Hospital in Kampong Trabek. There I took pictures of faces. I took thousands and thousands and thousands of pictures of faces.

*(The light around **SOPOAN** continues to expand, revealing even more pictures and **ROM CHANG**.)*

*(She stands a few feet behind **SOPOAN**, inspecting the array of photographs.)*

ROM CHANG. So many. So many faces, yes?

SOPOAN. Yes.

(He turns to look at her.)

ROM CHANG. Face front. You do not have permission to look at me when you answer for your crimes.

SOPOAN. I have no crimes.

ROM CHANG. I have witness accounts Sopoan. You commit economic sabotage. You infect the people with your memory sickness.

(He tries to look at her again.)

I said face front! What is rule ten?

SOPOAN. I –

ROM CHANG. Rule ten.

SOPOAN. If I disobey your regulations I shall get either ten lashes or five shocks of electric discharge.

ROM CHANG. So why do you disobey?

(Short pause.)

Look at the pictures Sopoan. Your face will be there soon.

(He doesn't.)

I said look at them.

SOPOAN. No.

*(**ROM CHANG** studies **SOPOAN** and then looks to the wall of pictures. Short pause.)*

ROM CHANG. Which is it?

SOPOAN. I don't know what –

ROM CHANG. Which picture?

(Beat.)

Do not make me get the wire.

SOPOAN. It is a feather.

ROM CHANG. I am losing my patience with you.

(Short pause.)

You can tell me Sopoan. You do not have to be afraid.

(No response:)

This one?

(She studies him, turns back to the wall.)

ROM CHANG. Which is it?

(Re: A picture.)

Ah. This one.

(She puts the picture in front of his face.)

ROM CHANG. This one is familiar to you?

SOPOAN. No.

ROM CHANG. No? You do not know her?

SOPOAN. No.

ROM CHANG. Good. Because I will tell you that I remember this one. I remember her because… I think she was very much like me.

(No response.)

She was a "new person" from the city. You can see this. But we are about the same age. Pretty. Do you think she is pretty Sopoan?

(Beat.)

I asked you a question.

SOPOAN. I –

ROM CHANG. Look at her.

*(**SOPOAN** does.)*

ROM CHANG. This girl is pretty, yes?

(No response.)

Answer.

SOPOAN. She is.

ROM CHANG. She was. Oh yes. I remember this one. These new people, they act so proud. But not this girl Sopoan. This girl was just…too sad. She had the memory sickness too you see.

(Beat.)

I do not have to tell you that our revolution has no use for a person like this. There is nothing to be done for a person like this. Do you understand?

SOPOAN. Yes.

ROM CHANG. Do you wish to know what became of her?

SOPOAN. No.

ROM CHANG. They took her to the yard. You have seen what happens in the yard?

(No response.)

The revolution reveals a coward, does it not?

SOPOAN. The revolution reveals a coward.

ROM CHANG. Oh yes. And I remember she... It was surprising. The guards watching. The boys swinging the pipes. The others around her begging, screaming, soiling themselves in the yard and she was so...still... It was surprising to me. And a man came from inside. And this man said that perhaps our revolution has some use for a person like this after all. And he held out his hand.

(Beat.)

There is still mercy you see. Brother Number One is merciful. Brother Number One has tenderness for all his children. Does he not?

SOPOAN. Brother Number One is merciful.

ROM CHANG. Yes. And I am merciful. And this man was merciful. He took her inside. And she asked them, to cure her sickness.

SOPOAN. No.

ROM CHANG. Yes. Because of some man. It was some man, you see. She lost him. Her husband. There is such sadness to love a man so much. She begged them to take her memory. And they did.

SOPOAN. No.

ROM CHANG. And she learned to be like them Sopoan. To do these things. But this girl was special you see. This girl, she learned to see inside. You have heard of this girl.

SOPOAN. No.

ROM CHANG. You cannot lie to me Sopoan. No one lies to me.

*(Short pause. She regards **SOPOAN** who looks down at the floor.)*

ROM CHANG. ...This girl had smooth pale skin. Do you remember a girl like that?

SOPOAN. No.

ROM CHANG. She was standing by the Monivong Bridge in her summer hat… The breeze from the river brought the smell of her hair down to you. What was it?… What was that smell?

SOPOAN. Hyacinth.

ROM CHANG. Yes… And one night, beneath the stars, you held her hand like a butterfly in yours. And it was the softest thing you ever did.

SOPOAN. Stop.

ROM CHANG. It was the last soft thing you ever did.

(Short pause.)

At night, when you hang from that rail alone, do you go to her Sopoan? In your memory. Do you still go?

SOPOAN. Yes.

*(**SOPOAN** looks up and meets **ROM CHANG**'s eyes.)*

ROM CHANG. What was her name?

SOPOAN. Chantrea… Your name. Chantrea.

ROM CHANG. She is gone. This girl does not remember you. Do you understand? She cannot remember you.

SOPOAN. I remember…

ROM CHANG. You do?

SOPOAN. I remember…how I held your hand.

(Short pause.)

ROM CHANG. Do not carry this. It hurts to carry this. Give this to me Sopoan. So you can forget.

SOPOAN. I want to remember.

ROM CHANG. No one wants to remember. No one.

SOPOAN. I will remember.

ROM CHANG. It is too heavy Sopoan.

SOPOAN. I will carry it with you.

(A beat. She looks at him.)

ROM CHANG. You wish to be useful to our revolution?

SOPOAN. Yes. I will be useful.

ROM CHANG. What will you do?

> (**SOPOAN** *reaches out and takes the camera from the table. He looks at it in his hands.* **SOPOAN** *takes his own picture as the lights fade to black.*)

End of Play

www.ingramcontent.com/pod-product-compliance
Lightning Source LLC
Chambersburg PA
CBHW071837290426
44109CB00017B/1844